BUSK

As A Mercenary Art

Or, How to Hustle A Bar

By

ALFIE

"King of the Street Conjurors"

All rights reserved. No portion of this material may be reproduced in any form or by any means, without the express written permission from the author or his agent, not no how, not no way.

PRINTED IN THE UNITED STATES OF AMERICA – 2012

Copyright © 2012 by the author, J. Paul Moore

Ion Drive Publishing,
Los Angeles

http://IonDrivePublishing.com

DEDICATED TO

JULES LENIER
AND
BILLY MCCOMB

Two gentlemen of magic from whom
I have learned more than I will ever
remember

Table of Contents:

About the Authors

Forward

1. Picking the Right Bar 2
2. Entering the Bar 5
3. Old Territory 8
4. Working the Crowd 9
      Alfie's Opening Coin Routine 11
      Side Bar 15
      Sample Routine 16
      Building the Tip 17
      Foreshadowing the Tip 17
      Turing the Tip 19
      The Re-Hash 21
      Moving On 23
5. Enemies of the Busker 24
6. Equipment 26
7. Angles 27
8. Permits and Licenses 28

9. Fees and Contracts 28
10. Unconnected Afterthoughts 29
11. Your Material 31
12. Your Edge 31
13. How to Work a Restaurant 32
14. Working the Street 38
15. Taxes 45
16. The Bottom Line 46
17. Alfie's Busking Vest 47
18. Summary 47
My Personal Guarantee 48

Reserve Stock

FORWARD

I've known "Alfie" (J. Paul Moore) for well over twenty years now. He can walk in to any situation and perform magic. Following that he will pass the hat and get enough money to live on.

The world is his oyster. He has proven over and over again that the role of the traveling magician can take him from one country to another and make many friends in the doing. This booklet gives you some of his secrets.

I sincerely look forward to ALFIE putting more of his ideas and figuring on paper.

We can learn a tremendous amount from the psychology and thinking which have gone into them and the trial and error required to produce the final result.

Billy McComb

About the Authors

Alfie, "King of the Street Conjurors" is the creation of American actor, J. Paul Moore. Alfie first surfaced on the streets of San Francisco circa 1970, in conjunction with the first Dickens Christmas Fair. After that he became one of the City's first Street Performers, and was the first to receive written permission to perform in The Cannery. ("We were still being thrown out of Ghirardelli Square.") Alfie could be found nightly busking the saloons and watering holes along Union Street. "Perry's was sort of my headquarters and I would branch out to Thomas Lords, The Mother Lode, and The Bus Stop, with occasional sorties up to Henry Afrika's or down to the Pierce Street Annex."

Alfie became the Resident Magician aboard the Queen Mary in Long Beach before moving on to a seven year run as the "Wizard of the Waterways" with Princess Cruises. A performing member of the world-famous Magic Castle in Hollywood since 1966, Alfie was awarded the Close-Up Magician of the Year by the Blackstone Ring of the International Brotherhood of Magicians in Cleveland, Ohio, where he held sway as House Magician for the popular nite-spot, Shooter's on-the-Water. While based in Las Vegas during the early 2000's Alfie performed as

Professor Marvel, the House Magician at the Rain Forest Café at MGM Grand and demonstrated magic for Houdini Magic in most of the major Casinos on the strip, continuing as pitchman for Houdini Magic at Disneyland. Alfie spent most of this century as a regular street performer with Uniiversal Studio's CityWalk before retiring to the Lake Arrowhead area, where he performs (2012) at the Lake Arrowhead Village.

J. Paul Moore has been a resident of Los Angeles/San Francisco for the better part of forty years, and has appeared in commercials, films (*The Prestige, Pirates of the Caribbean*) and television. For forty plus years he acted, wrote, directed and taught at the original Renaissance Pleasure Faires of California. J. Paul is also the author of *Guerrilla Theatre for Faires and Festivals*, a guide-book for performing environmental theatre. He and his former wife Sandy have three children, Ryan, Morgan and Courtney and two grandsons, Alexander and Conor J.

In addition to his Alfie character, Mr. Moore has created other characters for specific events such as Tip, The Wizard; Prospero, Court Magician to the Duke of Milan; the grifter, Doc Wiley; and of course Mssr. Robert-Houdin, the Illusionist for The Great Dickens Christmas Fair, now in its 44th year in San Francisco.

As Robert-Houdin at the Great Dickens Christmas Faire

On the Pacific Princess

Prospero

Montgomery Sneed

At the Magic Castle in Hollywood...

Busking As A Mercenary Art
OR,
How To Hustle A Bar

By ALFIE,
"King of the Street Conjurors"
A.K.A.
J. Paul Moore

Unless you are a unique individual indeed, the only pure motive for busking is to make money.

Sometimes you are not making the big bucks. This is affectionately known to the professional entertainer as "down time". Those times when you are seriously considering a "real job" that pays minimum wage, has a time clock and demands that you allow someone to inspect your urine, check your blood and sample your hair. With the ancient and noble art of busking you can easily make three times that much, to start, and it holds the promise of potential wealth. If you apply the principles laid out in this book and have any talent at all, you can maintain a steady weekly income that keeps the wolf from the door and allows you the freedom to pursue your career.

Of course, as an independent contractor you will need to take care of your taxes at year's end, so it would behoove you to keep some sort of record of your earnings and expenses, details of which we will touch upon in a later chapter.

The scenario, then, is this: The busker walks in to a bar, spends an hour or two doing magic for the troops and walks out with a pocket full of cash and the goodwill of all. Heading for another bar to do the same, sometimes you will encounter the High Roller and come away with big bucks, sometimes you will make zip. This book is to minimize the latter.

1. Picking the Right Bar

As your primary objective is to make money, you must, obviously, choose a bar frequented by people who have money to spend. As a general rule, the more expensive the bar the better your chances of doing well. A bar where professionals gather is also preferred as these people enjoy a higher disposable income and also have a courteous respect for your professionalism. Do not rule out the working man's neighborhood bar but do not look for the heavy spenders there. In truth you want two to five dollars from every one rather than a hundred from one person. Of course on those rare occasions when the full yard does come your way, savor the moment.

One way of picking a lucrative spot is to size up their parking lot. Rich people can dress like bums and poor folk can put on a good front, but generally, people drive the best car they can. If that parking lot is full of twenty-year-old rust buckets, you're not going to make very much money. If on the other hand, it is full of BMW's, Maseratis and Rolls Royces, you have found the Promised Land.

A few words here about the crowds, which vary drastically, even in the same bar, throughout the day: From approximately 11:30 A.M. to 2:00 PM is, of course, the lunch crowd which is usually in a hurry or busy discussing business or office politics. You will earn more ill will than money by bothering this crowd. Sleep in, revise your resume, work on your TV pilot, make those follow up phone calls. Saturday lunch or better yet, Sunday Brunch can work well for you, as this is a more leisurely time.

From 4:30 until around 7:00 PM is extended Happy Hour or whatever they are calling it these days. This can be a time of good pickings indeed. In this time frame you encounter people relaxing after the day's work, avoiding commuter traffic or just killing time before going home to face the wife/husband/kids/dog.

From 7:00 until 8:00 PM is usually pretty dead in the bar scene so this is a good time for you to get some dinner yourself. Often you can work a deal with the management for dinner. Personally I prefer to go elsewhere, have a nice dinner and leave a generous tip. I find this to be a fine psychological boost. By all means

<u>DO NOT SKIP DINNER</u> or you will pay dearly around 10:30 when the joint is jumpin' and you have no energy left. Make no mistake, busking is hard work and requires all the energy and concentration you can muster. Nobody tips someone to bring them down.

Prime time, like on TV, is from 8:00 to 11:00 PM. People are coming in to have a good time and, perhaps, meet someone. Your help with both will predispose them to tip you. Your energy kindles more energy in others and helps to establish a friendly buzz throughout the place; something unique is happening. As you perform, gradually including those gathering around, you act as a catalyst for conversation. You are doing a coin trick for two gals at the bar; two guys who are nearby notice something going on and move closer. You include them in your sphere as well as others who happen by. You ask people their names and use their names as you continue. This lets everybody know who everybody else is. When you leave, after allowing everyone the opportunity to tip you, the group is now on a more personal level, almost as though they have been properly introduced and they share a common topic of conversation. Those parties so interested now have the opportunity to develop relationships, buy one another drinks, chat, and eventually take a cottage by the sea. More about these groups later in "BUILDING THE TIP"

By 11:00 pm, especially in the singles bars, final moves are being made, and people are taking their last shots: it's do-or-die time. If they do not know who they are going home with by 11:30, chances are they are going home alone. DO NOT GET IN THEIR WAY AT THIS

TIME. Also, by this time, many in the crowd have had more than enough to drink and tend to get sloppy, dropping your cards, spilling their drinks, becoming rude and generally coming to resent you for being a free spirit who does not have to get up at 6:30 in the morning to go punch a time clock. I recommend a pleasant exit before any of this happens.

NAME THREE BARS WHERE YOU COULD TRY THIS STUFF OUT

1. _____
2. _____
3. _____

2. Entering The Bar

As a busker you are entirely dependent on your tips, so everything about you should be geared toward the bigger-than-life aspect of your performance. This extends to your appearance. The moment you walk into the bar, heads should turn, eyes look up and everyone who sees you should realize, immediately, that you are up to something. This is not to say you must be dressed in a clown suit with a neon hat (although this would probably work nicely) but there should be something distinctive about you. In the beginnings of Alfie, as a street conjuror in San Francisco, I wore a threadbare, formerly grand Dickensian outfit with battered and sewn back together top hat. In more recent times I have gone to the standard tux with tails although I use the occasional wizard robe or flim flam outfit.

Wear something distinctive to separate yourself from the crowd.

ENTER WITH ENERGY!!!

You are bringing power to the establishment. If you have not already obtained permission to work, immediately approach the bartender, unless he/she is swamped with work. In this case you could do a few tricks for the people waiting for their drinks at the bar. (Do not go for a tip at this time). Usually the bartender will leave you alone until getting caught up with the drink orders. By now he has seen that you are a pleasant fellow/fellowess who does magic. When you have his attention, briefly tell him your name as you hand him your card, tell him you are a traveling magician and may you do a little magic for the guests at the bar. Most times he will say, "Sure, go ahead". Sometimes he will refer you to the manager.

If you are referred to the manager, pick out a likely looking group of people and be doing some magic when the manager arrives. (Do not hustle these folks for a tip). He will be more disposed to letting you work if he sees a happy entertained group of customers when he walks up.

On the odd chance he says "NO", for whatever reason, thank him kindly, suggest, 'perhaps another time' and take your leave. Under no circumstances let him know that he is an unimaginative jerk who is missing a rare opportunity. This will always work against you. Just move on. You can't win them all.

When the manager or bartender DOES give you permission, work the room comfortably for an hour or so, as instinct dictates, and take your leave, bidding all (especially the manager or bartender) a fine farewell. You want to leave on an up note, not after you have become "old hat".

Move on the next bar on your list and try the same routine all over again. Your goal, if you are staying in one place for any length of time, is to establish three bars where you are welcome to perform. Once you have set these places up, unless you have done something stupid, like hitting on the bartender's girl-friend, you will be welcome any time you stop by and will never need to ask permission again.

By the by, for what it is worth, avoid franchised places like TGI Friday or Lone Star and places like that. They are usually corporate-run and the managers have no authority to let you work. You might see if they can get an approval from on high but that could take some time.

Ultimately and ideally, you have set up three watering holes where your genius is appreciated. This should keep you busy all night. When one peters out, move on to the next. By the end of the evening you should have three to four times as much cash in your pocket as you could make working all day for wages. Of course for those of you on the constant move, you could cultivate any bar you run across and never go back to the same one twice.

3. Old Territory

Let us suppose you are entering a bar where you have already been given clearance. Enter with power and energy. If your timing is right there should already be, at least, a small crowd. Wave knowingly to a group of people toward the back of the crowd (whether there is anyone you know there or not). You are actually playing to everyone between you and the back of the bar. Move confidently toward the back, noting who has tuned in to you on the way. As you pass this person or group, pause, as though the person has somehow attracted your attention. Say something like: "Say. You didn't happen to bring a deck of cards, did you? Ah well, we'll use mine," (launching into your opening card routine) or "Have you seen that old coin trick where...." Gradually warm to the group, dropping the temporary pause attitude and continue your act. It is very important that you get a good reaction from this first group as it sets a tone, in the mind of the people who are noticing from afar, that something neat is going on. This first group is your springboard to the other people in the bar. Get as much bounce out of them as possible. Get them to laugh and applaud, even cheer and whistle.

If you sense that you are going into the toilet with this group immediately conclude whatever trick you are on. Do not hit them for a tip, wish them well, and move on with a cheery smile to the next likely looking group and start over. If you die a death three times in a row, you are either in a morgue or perhaps not cut out to be a busker. Leave the bar and give some serious thought to that straight job.

NAME THREE JOBS YOU COULD BE DOING INSTEAD OF BUSKING

1._____

2._____

3._____

4. Working the Crowd

You are headed for the "Soft Touch Bar and Grill", a likely establishment where you have already scoped out and obtained the blessings of the management. It is a Friday evening, about eight o'clock, and as you approach the place you note, through the window, that, sure enough, a goodly crowd has already gathered, waiting for fate to strike. Getting your coin in to palm position you step into the doorway and pause for a moment to look around. You are actually posing for a moment so that Mac can nudge Mick with a ... "Hey, check this guy out." In this time you are also scanning the crowd looking for your first Mark. Spot him quickly, wave at some indiscriminate spot beyond him and begin your move in that direction. (Do not pose overly long in the doorway or you will not only look like you are posing, but someone may come in and rudely tell you to stop blocking the doorway).

Moving past your Mark, you let him catch your eye, pause, move back in to his sphere, allowing him to think that he has somehow attracted your attention. As you enter his sphere of influence, you encounter the **15 seconds to doom** aspect of your performance. That is about how long you have before the Mark is either intrigued by what you are doing or turns away muttering "Oh shit, a magician."

Start, then, with something quick and good. I start with a coin trick that leads into a one-coin routine. It is designed to catch and pique their interest with quality sleight-of-hand. I know, when I reach the end of the routine, if I should remain with this group or move on. I will put the routine down here as an example of how this works. Although you may feel free to use the routine as is, you will be much better served to tap your own creative genius and come up with an opening that fulfills the same purpose: To grab and hold attention in a pleasing manner.

ALFIE'S OPENING COIN ROUTINE

1. (Coin in classic palm position, display the other hand open), "Have you seen that old trick where the magician waves his hand and produces a silver coin?" (Simply drop the coin into your closing hand as you wave). Most times the Mark is not even watching the hand at this point and is somewhat surprised to look down and see a coin in your previously empty hand. Oft times he will say "Wait a minute, do that again" *{Big shiny coins, like silver dollars, are more impressive than half dollars. I use an 1899 Walking Liberty Silver Dollar. The coin itself commands attention.}*

2. "Do you realize that is just the opposite of the one where you wave your hand and it disappears... the coin, not the hand. (Vanish the coin back in to the classic palm position). I don't do that one - I don't do it very well. I'll show you the one I do." At this point you should have piqued his attention and perhaps a few more folk as well and extracted a chuckle.

3. "This is the one I do: I use the invisible pocket in the hand," (drawing the right index finger along the life line of the left hand). "Close the hand. Turn it over, press the back

of the hand, and the coin slides right out of the invisible pocket (revolve production). At this point the Mark usually nudges his friend who has been studying the liquor bottle labels on the bar back and says, "Hey Charlie, look at this." You continue, "Just your basic coin trick, really."

At this point you have used up your 15 seconds and should have generated at least a mild interest. By this point, if I do not recognize an appreciation for what I am doing I may well cut it short and move on the next Mark. Use something like: "My name is _____, I am a traveling magician, I'll be wandering about. If you would care to see a bit of magic just give me a wave. Have a grand night." And move on with no hard feeling all around. Not everyone you encounter is up for it so wish them well and move on.

4. Most likely they are with you now as you begin a coin roll. "This, of course, is the coin roll. Pretty. Useless, but pretty. That's what the wife says about me... Pretty useless." During this clever patter you have been rolling the coin across your fingers, dropping it in to the left hand.

"The important thing is to keep your eye on the coin. (Here you appear to finish the roll by dropping the coin in to your left hand but actually retain it in your right hand. Closing the left hand you draw it up and away as you say, "You'd be surprised how many people look away from the coin." (As you open your left hand to show the coin gone, the right hand gets the coin rolling again so that when they look back they see the coin in mid-roll). "I'll go slowly; don't let that happen here."

5. By now you should have 5 or 6 people suitably impressed and willing to let you continue. DO SO. "Now keep your eye on the coin. If you look away, I could make an elephant disappear." (Toss the coin in to the left hand, as before, but this time really toss it and make it look (subtly) like you have palmed it with the right hand. People are not stupid. By now they are on to you and know that the coin is palmed in your right hand. Some people will actually grab your hand but at the very least someone will look at it. Open the right hand): "See, that's what I mean, you've got to keep your eye on the coin. Otherwise you miss the whole trick." (Toss the coin back into the right hand).

6. "In fact, do me a favor; keep an eye on the wrist so you know it doesn't go up the sleeve or under the watch. *Time for the Coup de Gras.* (Seem to toss the coin into your left hand but keep it classic-palmed in the right hand and, under the misdirection of indicating the left wrist, lap it into your waiting and rigged vest). *{What? You don't have a waiting and rigged vest? See the Alfie's Busking Vest section.}* "A wave of the hand, a snap of the fingers, and the coin vanishes in to thick air." (Show both hands empty). "I learned the trick in L.A," (or the nearest big

smoggy city): "Feel free to applaud if you like." It is most helpful if you get your crowds to applaud. This signals to everyone at a distance that something good is happening and their curiosity will be piqued.

During this routine I have built my crowd, or The Tip as it is called, from the one or two people I started with to a half dozen or more. They are now suitably impressed and ready to allow me their interest for a few more minutes. I often, believe it or not, go in to Hot Rod at this point because it is pretty, appeals to the ladies and gets them in to the act. (My Hot Rod routine is printed in "RESERVE STOCK, V.S.O.P." later in this book).

After this short interlude I usually launch into card tricks because as old-hat as they may seem to we magician types, you would be amazed at how many people have never seen good, close-up, sleight-of-hand card tricks. And they love them.

I also like moving in to card tricks, not only because it is a minimum of equipment to carry around and is immediately identifiable, but because they afford the opportunity to employ many members of what should now be a sizable crowd. The more you use their names and keep them involved, the more fun they will have, and the more disposed they will be toward tipping you when the time comes.

SIDE BAR

From time to time one of your Marks will want to show you a card trick. Give your reaction some thought. There are pro's and con's. Think about your crowd. Are they all buddies of his? If so, perhaps give him a shot. 1. It makes him a part of the show. 2. You will look better by comparison, and 3, you just might learn something, either in the way of a new trick or a different presentation. True, you will endure a plethora of hemorrhoid tricks, but what the hell.

On the other hand, if it is a varied audience, this guy may be incredibly boring and blow off your hard won crowd. He may also drop your cards in a puddle of beer. Size up the situation and make your decision. You might suggest that you would love to see his trick after you have finished. You might even be able to use his trick to launch into a re-hash after you have collected your tips. It can be tricky (pun Intended).

On Stage at Sea, aboard the Pacific Princess

SAMPLE ROUTINE

Outline below a routine of six effects you already know. Include a line of patter.

SAMPLE:

        <u>effect</u>   <u>patter</u>

    coin routine . . . . economic instability

    jumping card . . . . the Olympics

    floating elephant . . . . my last trip to Punjow

1._____
2._____
3._____
4._____
5._____
6._____

Professor Marvel performs the Floating Elephant in MGM's Rain Forest Café, Las Vegas.

Building the Tip

As you continue through your card routine, or whatever you have set to do next, continue to expand the sphere. Spot the guy who is observing from a few feet away and have him shuffle the cards. Notice the girls who are looking over your shoulder. Step back and bring them in to the group. Soon you are playing to a dozen or more people. This constitutes a nice-size group for close-up walk-around work. About five to ten minutes of good magic should pull ten to twenty dollars out of this group, at a minimum. As you can repeat this comfortably four or five times in an hour, you can see the potential to outstrip working for wages. Do this two or three nights a week and you should have no problem making the boat payment.

Foreshadowing the Tip

You have completed your coin routine and made an inroad toward building a crowd. You have moved on to the card tricks and built a respectable tip. After about three card tricks, at least one of which should be very impressive, you should let the audience know (in a pleasant way) that you are, indeed, a busker, and will be accepting tips. This should be done as their interest is on the rise, not when you are all done and they can easily slip away. This can be done in a number of ways. Here is one: (putting your cards away), "Card tricks get old after a while. Allow me to show you something that borders on magic.

Does anyone have a five-dollar bill I might borrow for a moment or two? I stress the term 'borrow'. I never keep anything that is not offered, I am a magician and not a thief, and I don't run that fast anymore (not for five bucks). "Ah, thank-you, a borrowed bill." Do a good trick with the borrowed bill. (not your best, but good). Perhaps turn it in to a one-dollar bill *(do not turn it in to A Hundred-Dollar Bill or they will think that you do not need the tip)* with patter along these lines:

"Being an itinerate magician of the open road, I do work strictly for tips. Occasionally the odd Five Dollar Bill comes my way. If I take that home and my wife sees it she will squander it on something foolish... like food or shelter. So what I do on the way home is to alter the appearance of the bill by folding it up and re-arranging the molecular structure, so that when she goes through my pockets she will say (showing the now-one dollar bill), 'I guess he didn't do very well, he only made it home with a dollar.'" (Look slightly askance at the donor as you say to the crowd), "The gentleman is amazed but not amused. Not to worry, when she leaves in the morning I will change the dollar back to its original state. That way I am able to keep snow tires on the Lamborghini." (Display fiver). "The original Five Dollar Bill. Your bill, sir," (handing the bill back). Often the Mark will thank you and say keep it.

"Thank you kindly sir," (addressing the crowd). "It's not for me you understand, it's for the children... My children... I told my daughter if I did well she could get that little tattoo she has her heart set on." Tuck the bill in your jacket breast pocket with a little sticking out as a "tip me" flag.

Continue with your performance. This is a good spot for a filler trick. You have a crowd, they are interested; time for something pretty. I am particularly fond of the Michael Ammar *Magic by Gosh* 3-D Multi-plying Rabbits. Far better than Sponge Balls because THEY ARE BUNNIES!

TURNING THE TIP

After your filler trick and perhaps one more minor miracle, you want to move into the most important part of your act. GETTING THE MONEY. Try this:

"Folks, you have been very kind to watch my little act. I would like to leave you with a minor miracle. Does anyone have a One Hundred Dollar Bill I might borrow? (This should get at least a snicker. On the odd chance that some foolish soul does offer you a One Hundred-Dollar Bill, take it and continue. Most times it will just get a laugh). Does anyone have a Fifty Dollar Bill I might borrow? A twenty? A ten? Okay, we're getting in to the cheap tricks now... Who's got a buck?" (Aside from getting you a bill to work with, this interlude gets people reaching for the wallets, opening their purses and thinking about money). The first step to getting their money IN to your pocket is to get it OUT of their pocket.

Take whatever bill you get and float it in the air. What do you mean you don't do a floating bill!? LEARN ONE!!! Use the Munari U.F.O. hook up, use Kennedy's, an I.T.R., or any one of a number of rigs. Any floatation will blow them away and send them scrambling for their wallets. I like the Munari system because you do not need an anchor and you can use it with a credit card for the occasional Mark who says, jokingly," Do you take Master Card?"

Finish the trick, and say: "Feel free to applaud if you like." (I stress again how helpful it is to get people applauding, cheering, stomping on the floor, etc.). As you unroll the bill, say... "Thank you very much, that concludes my performance. Any donations you might care to make will be gratefully accepted." Hand back the bill as you take off your hat. (You *are* wearing a hat are you not? Very handy for collecting tips). If you cannot handle a hat, no matter; just accept the tips as they come and tuck them in your jacket breast pocket. Now don't just stand there. Patter along as people are giving. Take a few minutes here to chat, listen to their stories about the magician they knew in the Army, hand out business cards. This keeps you in the area for those who have been slow to tip but have decided they would like to. Let them know that you will be around for a while. They may want to tip you but only have a twenty dollar bill and need to get change. They will often come up to you later and stuff a bill in your pocket. (They will not do this if you have insulted them for being cheap). When you feel you have collected all the tips you are going to get, unload the hat to your pocket and move on or Re-Hash as obvious instinct dictates.

On the odd chance that you finish up and no one in the crowd is forthcoming with a tip, do not show offense. No muttering of "Cheap so and so," or "Wassa, matter? Ain't ya gonna tip me?" Make your pleasant farewells, leave your card and carry on. Belabor the point no further. Maybe the folk have no cash and are living on plastic, or they need change and will catch up with you later. Maybe they are dense. Whatever, keep your thoughts to yourself and move on. Go complain to the rest-room attendant if you must, but do not put out any negative energy in public.

THE RE-HASH

There is the theory that the best crowd to get money out of is the crowd you have already got money out of. I have not often found this to be true, but often enough that you should consider the possibility.

After you have collected your tips and given out your cards, assess the situation. Did most people come in toward the end of your act? Have they been roaring with appreciation? Are they encouraging you to continue? Did someone flash a roll? If the answer to enough of these questions is yes, you may want to start up again with the same crowd. Different stuff, of course. Perhaps a gambling routine: three-card-monte, three-shell game, a cheating-at-cards routine. If you plan to do a gambling sequence, it would be good to photo copy some small sized fake money with your picture and phone number on it so you can give it to the Marks to play with. The routine is much stronger when the audience actually has a wager of some sort. Need I say it? Do not let them bet real money <u>under any circumstances</u>. That will immediately elevate you from the level of charming entertainer to thieving cheat, and could well get carted off to the local cooler.

LIST THREE EFFECTS OR A ROUTINE YOU COULD USE FOR A RE-HASH

1._____

2._____

3._____

Moving On

If your current crowd does not seem worthy of the re-hash, you will want to move on to another area. If the joint is crowded you might spot a likely looking Mark on the edge of the group to which you have been playing. Move in that direction, make eye contact, and start your routine all over again. This will carry you eight to ten feet from where you were working, and you can begin to build a new tip. As this is a brand new crowd there is no need to use new material. You can do the same routine, nearly word-for-word, all over again. (I have made a decent living for nearly fifty years using nothing more than a silver dollar, a deck of cards, some thumb tips and a few simple pocket tricks).

Work the new crowd and move on. Once you have played out the obvious areas of the bar and Marks are getting difficult to spot you can do one of two things:

1. Take a break and have a soda water or a soft drink at the bar. This gives you a chance to relax and gives anyone the opportunity to approach you with a million dollar T.V. offer. It also keeps you visible for those who may have been slow to tip.

2. Take your leave and head for another bar. If you line up three bars where you will be welcome, they will keep you busy through the night. You might even return to a bar later in the evening.

5. Enemies of the Busker

NEGATIVE ATTITUDE Nothing will work against you as effectively as a negative attitude on your part. Belligerence, antagonism, sarcasm, impatience and the whole menu of negative attitudes are not compatible to winning tips. Keep your real life feelings to your self and play the things that work: good cheer, humor, agreement, diplomacy, and escapist entertainment.

Without a doubt you will encounter negativity in some of the people you meet. Do your best to turn it around or get off the subject. If you are unable to do so, finish up, wish them well and move on to a new Mark. You are not there to change the world or dwell upon man's inhumanity to man. Your job is to offer a momentary escape from the realities of the day and thereby make some money. You will not make a dime by starting an argument or even being in the area of any discord! Keep your personal opinions to yourself and avoid anything of conflict or controversy.

LOUD MUSIC Since your patter and one-on-one interaction with the audience is a major part of the experience, avoid bars where a band is playing or recorded music is being blasted. The energy it takes to overcome this competition will drain you very quickly. When the music starts it is your cue to take your leave. Of course you might hang out and do some work on the breaks, but waiting for breaks is lost time which could well be spent elsewhere.

ALCOHOL While the effects of alcohol can be very beneficial to you when consumed by the Mark, it will do you no good to drink along with him. Many a fine magician has been done in by that oft-heard question: "Can I buy you a drink?" Thank him kindly but point out that it makes the hand slower than the eye and you would only end up fooling yourself. Perhaps at the end of the evening you might allow someone to buy you a drink but until then avoid it like the plague. The Mark will not be offended and it frees up more money for your tip.

DRUGS I make no effort to dictate what personal vices you should abstain from in your private life, but I can not state too strongly: DO NOT USE DRUGS WHILE WORKING. They have many drawbacks; they throw your timing off, sap your energy and can get you tossed in the local pokey. But most of all, they put you on a different level of reality from the people for whom you are working. As a busker you must continually relate to the elements around you. Keep all the wits about you that you can. Bear in mind the old lyric *"I got stoned and I missed it."* 'Nuff said?

DRUNKS Drunks are great to work for, up to a point. They can be funny, exuberant, cheerful, supportive and generous. When they have crossed over the line into sloppy, belligerent, and semi-comatose, they cease to be worth your effort. Although you may be able to deal with them just fine, the rest of the crowd can't, and they will begin to find ways of getting away. So should you.

BIG SCREEN TV Just briefly, if you walk in to a bar with a big screen T.V. on a Monday night during football season, you are not going to make a dime. However, if the local team wins you might cash in on the celebrations after the game.

USE THE AUDIENCE as much as possible. Let them shuffle the cards, hold out their hand, wave the wand, examine the rope, etc., etc. It makes them part of the act, a center of attention and most importantly it keeps them from slipping away. Use their names often. (Oh yes; do not do things that embarrass the spectator or make them look stupid. I am amazed at how often I see magicians do this. Guess how much money these people will give you).

USE FAMILIAR OBJECTS as well as the occasional exotic prop: coins, cards, bills, napkins, swizzle sticks, the Aztec Mummy Case you just happen to have in the van.

Far and away your most useful weapon is your wit, charm, and ability to relate to people. Be interested in them. LISTEN. Let them get their lines out.

6. Equipment

I reiterate and even mention again: KEEP IT TO A MINIMUM. Stick to the things you can repeat over and over again without resetting. Scotch and Soda is a powerful, if somewhat overused, trick but you have to scurry off with your bang ring every time to reset. Try Hopping Half.

Load up several thumb tips with various denominations of bills, silks etc.. Use cards, coins, rope if you must, rings, keys (be wary of what rings you use with Ring Flight. It is embarrassing to have to search the barroom floor for a lost diamond setting).

While I compliment and admire those of you slick enough to do a watch steal, DON'T! The opportunity for disaster is staggering. You could drop or damage the watch. It could get stepped on. The guy could catch you and take you for a thief (not at all helpful). Even worse, you could get caught up in the moment and forget to give it back. It has happened.

Sponge Rabbits is much better than Sponge Balls because they are cute little rabbits and it gives you an opening for that Mark who says, "Hey, can you pull a rabbit out of your..." Learn lots of things to do with borrowed bills

7. ANGLES

Just a few words about one of the most important considerations of performance magic. Quite obviously you will be working partially or completely surrounded on most occasions. Naturally, your selection of material must be angle-proof. Be aware of and rely heavily upon the opportunities for misdirection. A busy bar has all kinds of opportunities.

May I also suggest that red-backed cards are less easily spotted in your palm from across the room than are blue ones.

8. Permits and Licenses

Over the 40 + years that I have been a Busker, I have never been asked to show a license or permit of any kind. I am certain, however, if you were to go to any government office and inquire, some helpful soul would be happy to refer you to Window B in the office across the street, where you would be able to fill out Form W123456789.1AA ½ in triplicate, and submit it along with the blood of your first-born for their approval. The choice is yours.

9. Fees and Contracts

Personally I prefer not to charge the establishment a fee and definitely do not want the restrictions of a contract. Busking is transient by nature and I do not want to be obligated to show up at any particular time on any particular night. I may have a gig. I may go off on a cruise-ship or just want to see the kids play Easter Eggs in the school pageant. Once you accept a fee you are working for them. A BUSKER WORKS FOR HIMSELF!

That said, there is also much to be said for being the "House Magician". If you are going to be in one area for any length of time you might want to sell some local restaurant owner on the idea of table magic for his dining guests. This usually works out as a 3-4 hour shift. Estimate what you might make busking and charge the house something around that figure. You will still get some tips but should back off on the hard sell of foreshadowing and turning the tip. I have found it is good to say, "Courtesy of the house," once, then take the money if they insist. You may still do tricks with borrowed bills and let things take their own course. You also might work a deal for dinner after the shift.

Working tables in a restaurant is an entirely different situation than working a bar. I have added a small section further on in the book to address the considerations of the table magician.

10. UNCONNECTED AFTER-THOUGHTS

YOU AS THE TIPPER Take care of the people around you. Just as you make your money on tips, so do most of the workers in the bar. The barman will most likely give you your soft drinks for free. – TIP HIM. If you use the facilities – TIP THE ATTENDANT. If the waitress turns you on to a lucrative table – TIP HER. If you use the parking valet – TIP THEM. Perhaps I belabor the point...

STAY OUT OF THE WAITER/WAITRESS'S WAY

After all, the house's business is to sell and serve food. If you slow down that process you cost the house money (not an endearing quality), and they will not be glad to see you come back. You might want to talk to the service personnel and let them know you will be happy to help cover any delays. (Tragedy in the kitchen, lost orders, fight with the Chef, etc.). Remember that people are hungry/thirsty. It is the unwise Wizard who comes between the guest and his drink.

BUSINESS CARDS If you plan to be in the area for any length of time, it would behoove you to make up some business cards with your contact information. You will pick up some private work which is always helpful. Keep the card simple with just your name, title and phone, fax and/or email. Perhaps a clever graphic of some sort. I have expended as much as $1.00 per card for fancy 3-D color cards, and I have picked up just as much work, if not more, by scribbling my number down on a napkin. Remember the card is just for them to know how to get a hold of you. You can send them that spectacular promo-pac later. Give your cards out like water. You never know when it will pay off. It also helps to keep you in the tip area while you pass them out. Also, collect as many of their cards as possible for your mailing list.

DO NOT WEAR EXPENSIVE or expensive-looking jewelry. The Mark will think you have more money than he does (which you probably do).

11. YOUR MATERIAL

Quick, strong and portable are the by-words. As mentioned earlier, you will have about 15 seconds on your opening shot to catch their attention. After that you may do some things that take a little longer but long and involved effects rarely hold attention long enough to be worthwhile. "Out of this Universe" for example, is a powerful effect, but you will rarely be able to hold a crowd long enough to finish it. Any effect which requires a lengthy attention span becomes more difficult as the evening gets later. There are exceptions, of course, but do not rely on anything long or complicated as part of our standard routine.

12. YOUR EDGE

The crowded, lively, and oft times dimly-lit bar is fraught with opportunity for the observant busker. Keep your eyes alert for open purses, pockets and bags into which you might load coins, duplicate or palmed cards, small ceramic elephants. This is the ideal place to try out that invisible thread you have been afraid to use. (By the way, while doing your floating whatever, be very aware that some will try to grab the prop or pass their hand through the thread. Be ready to deal with this). It is said that when Harry Blackstone Sr. would take his floating light bulb into the audience, he would kick anyone in the shins who got too close.

Work with the waiters and barmen if they are up for it and have the time. Slip the palmed, signed card off to a passing waiter, he gives it to the barman who slips it into their drink or wallet on the bar, under the glass, wherever, while the Mark is busy watching you not find his card.

13. How to Work a Restaurant

Whereas the bar is pretty much free-form and improvisational in its format, working a restaurant situation is very different, and requires some specific timing. When to approach the table, when not to; how long to stay, what material to use. Who do you look for, who do you avoid. Should I negotiate a salary or just work for tips?

Let us start with the salary idea. The House Magician position at a restaurant is usually an ongoing thing requiring a commitment on your part. You would be well-served to negotiate a salary of some sort. Ideally, equal to what you would expect to make on tips and then decline tips when they are offered saying "Thank you, it's a courtesy of the house." HOWEVER, you should only decline the tip once. If they insist, for heaven's sake do not stand there and argue with them. It would be rude to spurn their generosity.

You might also try negotiating a guarantee of some sort. The house guarantees you $50.00 and anything over that is yours. (Figure arbitrary).

A good way to start out is to tell the owner or manager that you will do a few days for free, just for tips to see how he/she likes the idea. This also gives you a chance to see what kind of tips can be expected and you can set your rate respectively.

<u>OK, YOU GOT THE GIG</u> The very first thing you must bear in mind when you work a restaurant is: THEY CAME THERE TO EAT! I know we would like to think it was our wonderful reputation for quality magic that brought them in. but NO, THEY CAME TO EAT!! Do not get in the way of the service. If you are in the middle of your best trick and the servers approach the table with hot plates, BACK OFF. Say something about dinner appearing out of thin air, "as if by magic." The customer will appreciate it and most of all, the server with the armload of hot plates will appreciate it. You can always pick up the trick again later, or if not, so be it.

WHEN TO APPROACH THE TABLE As a general rule it is best not to approach the table until they have placed their order with the waiter. Unless, of course the waiter has asked you to fill for a bit while they get caught up. Once the order is in, you should have a good ten minutes to work the table before the entrée arrives. Yes, there will be salad, soup and appetizers, but nothing that should require much diversion from your performance. I think it is best to be done and gone by the time the main course arrives.

Most likely, if it is a busy restaurant, you will not be able to get to all the tables before the main course, so the next best time is as they are winding down and considering or having dessert. You may have been interrupted in your act with the arrival of dinner. Dessert time is a good time to swing back by and float that borrowed $5.00 bill.

WHO TO APPROACH, WHO NOT TO A certain amount of sensitivity and common sense is to be encouraged here. As you stroll the restaurant you will feel the mood of the tables as you pass. Is someone looking at you inquisi-tively? Move in. Do they look bored? Go perk them up. Are they calling you over? In like Flynn. Are they a couple looking longingly into each others' eyes and speaking in hushed tones? Leave them alone. Are they being regaled by a good story? Leave them alone. Business discussion going on? Leave them alone. You are there to entertain, not interrupt.

WHAT KIND OF MATERIAL Do remember that this is an eating situation. Do not use anything gross or unappetizing. I actually knew of a fellow who would produce a pile of fake dog poop on the guests' breakfast table. Need I comment on this?

Much like the bar situation, your material should be quick, clean and specific. Do not put props on the table as you may be interrupted at any moment with dinner. Also, just as in the bar or any venue where you hope to garner some tips, you should do things that get the money out of their pocket. I usually borrow a $5.00 bill and do the story about hiding my tips from the wife by turning the $5 into a $1. I turn it back into the $5.00 and hand it back. Usually the tip comes right there and I encore by floating it in air.

NO TIP??? When you come to the end of your routine and no tip is forthcoming, do not let it phase you. Wish them a cheery good evening and move on. There are many reasons why people do not tip. Often they do not have change and will approach you later. Some people do not believe in tipping. Some folks do not even think about tipping you. (You can help cure this ignorance in your patter). Also, some folks just don't have the money. Most times you will get your tip. If this is not the case, you might consider looking for a restaurant with a better clientele.

USE THE WAITERS If they are up for it, and have the time, the waiters can be very helpful by slipping cards or other props under a plate being served or mixed in with their change, or any number of clever things. Usually waiters/waitresses like being a part of the show and will be more than happy to help out – unless they think you are cutting into their tips, which is why tipping out can be beneficial. Also, let them know that if they need a filler at a table because of a mix up in the kitchen or other snafu, you will be glad to be of help.

KIDS, KIDS AND MORE KIDS Also, unlike the saloon situation, you will encounter a lot of kids in the restaurant scenario. FEAR NOT. Many kids are actually well behaved and polite. Many are not. Try to remember, when the kid tells everybody how you just did your trick, that he is a kid and that is just the way it is with kids. Mostly include the kids in what you are doing. Have them wave the wand and say the magic words. Let them appear to have done the trick when possible. Not only does this make it much more fun for the kids, the parents will be appreciative.

Be aware, however, that this kid may well grab your floating whats-it. Keep it away from him. No need to do any kicking *ala* Blackstone, just be on your toes.

Parents whose kids have been delighted tend to tip well.

ABANDON TABLE! ABANDON TABLE! Once the check hit's the table, do not approach it again. The name of the restaurant game is TURNOVER. Once the guest has finished dinner, there is no benefit in encouraging them to linger over-long. True you do not want to rush people. Still, the house, the waiter, and you, all want to see a new customer at that table as soon as possible. If the people are leaving and did not tip you, you could put yourself in a position to say goodnight to them as they leave. It is a last-ditch effort but sometimes works.

TIPPING OUT Generally you are not expected to tip out to anyone. However, if someone has been particularly helpful to you, be generous. Did a waiter turn you on to a good table? Tip him. Did the waitress go out of her way to help you do a certain trick? Tip her. If you used anyone's services; barman, custodian, valet, etc., tip them. It will come back to you thrice-fold.

IN CONCLUSION Being the House Magician in a quality restaurant can be a very lucrative arrangement indeed. Not only will you make a comfortable cash flow, you will make contacts for the 4th of July Company Picnic, the Corporate Christmas Party, that special something for Bob's 40th birthday. Keep plenty of business cards and give them out like water. You never know.

14. Working the Street

This is, without a doubt, the most challenging venue available to the Busker. In a bar or restaurant, folk are at their leisure and awaiting serendipity. On the street, however, people are on their way somewhere, and you must somehow stop them and hold them and entertain them long enough to deserve a tip. Not an easy task: you also have ambient noise (sirens, car horns, the hustle and bustle of the town), and the variety of personalities you will encounter is staggering.

ANECDOTE: Twice I have had my crowd run off by religious fanatics, crying "Do not watch this man, he is a tool of the Devil!" once at 3rd Street Promenade in Santa Monica, and again in Old Pasadena.

As the zealots at the Promenade were disbursing the audience, my son Ryan, who was staying with me on his way to full Punkdom, struck up a conversation with one of them on the subject of "A woman's right to choose" and began strolling away down the Promenade. They followed him en-masse, and I was able to gather a new crowd and continue.

So, take a deep breath and prepare to enter the Crucible.

As with any business, a major key is "Location, Location, Location." You must have considerable foot traffic, and preferably be in a place frequented by tourists. For some seven or eight years, I have had the good fortune to perform in the streets of Universal Studio's City Walk, where thousands of folk pass by of any given evening. (Please note that some places do not allow street performers, and some require a permit which is usually easily obtained; check with fellow street performers, if possible).

As well as location, weather also plays an important part. Obviously, rain is a no-go if you are outside (it's hard to do card tricks in the rain), and extreme heat or cold work against you as well.

Your look, both costume-wise and set-up-wise, should be attractive, but not so opulent that the mark thinks you are wealthy.

You must also have an easily accessible yet not-easily-stealable receptacle for your tips. Prime the pump with a little "salt", ie. a couple of bills; not only to show where the money goes, but also to suggest an amount. I find two singles and a five work well, encouraging those five dollar tips which go so far toward making your evening.

Although I have only rarely had anyone try to steal my hat (the money receptacle), it can happen, and there are desperate people out there. You have drunks and druggies, people who do not speak English, and of course the homeless (whom, if you treat them with respect and a couple of sly bucks once in a while, will be very supportive).

Regarding your material, the most important thing, as always, is ANGLES! Working the street you have no control over your crowd and they will surround you and many will even practically sit on your shoulder trying to figure out your stuff. Unless you are using a backdrop, which is a hassle to carry around, do not do anything that flashes from the back.

As far as material goes, Quick, Clean, and Pretty are the key words. If you have some kids around, you're going to adapt your material to them: again, play to the children and their parents will be grateful.

There are thousands of street performers and many among them magicians. Each act will have its own evolved way of working the crowd. I will lay out some of the things that have worked for me over my years of Busking.

I do a small, close-up act of about 8 to 10 minutes, then "turn the tip" and start over with the newest arrivals, or as soon as possible. I do not do any tricks that a 12 year old couldn't do with 30 years of practice.

For example, I carry 3 or four different color "Hot Rods". It is a pretty, flashy trick that delights little girls. (And if you get one with diamonds it will delight the, not-so-little girls). That trick will hold a couple of kids long enough for passers-by to notice something is going on. OLD ADDAGE: "NOTHING ATTRACTS A CROWD LIKE A CROWD."

Sometimes I will start with a card trick for an interested gentleman or couple. The idea is to hold as many people as you can so that a growing crowd fills in behind them.

I may do a thumb-tip silk trick, tied to the patter of "A small silk scarf, once actually worn by Tinker Belle's younger sister...whom I dated in the late 60's...I think... anyway..." This trick is basically waving a flag that says, "Hey, look over here!" It is also very pretty and plays well to the kids.

Perhaps I should mention that I like to play to kids when they are present, including them in the act by having them hold the wand, or by waving their hands, saying the magic words, holding on to Mrs. Bunny, or one of my others kid-friendly tricks. There are several reasons for this: First of all, it delights them and they glow. Their eyes get *sooo* big. That energy coming back from them will keep you going for a long time. Second of all, their parents are delighted to see their children glow, and they, most likely, will tip you.

After Tinker Belle's scarf, I should have a crowd of a dozen or so, and I will launch into a few card tricks; played to the children if they are there, but more importantly, to the adults so that they will see some good sleight-of-hand.

Now that we have a nice crowd of 15-20 people I make my first mention of tips by including it in my magic chant, which comes while doing some sort of color change, or the 7-CARD stop effect outlined later in this worthy tome. Here's my chant:

"NAMAYOHORENGAYKEOTIMOTHYLEARY-BROWNRICESPARECHANGELRONHUBBARDAN-THONYROBBINS... I WORK FOR TiiiIIIPS!" (Gesture toward tip receptacle; then, as an aside to someone in crowd), "Subtle, huh?"

IMPORTANT: Keep your tip receptacle available to the audience at all times. Many people will have to go but would like to tip you before they do. Make it easy for them. – Thank-you's and variations there-of cannot be over-used.

After about three good card tricks you should have solidified the crowd. They are intrigued, interested or just trapped in the middle of the crowd and are ready for you to continue. At this point, I go to the Bunny Trick (Multiplying Rabbits) and say, "I think we have enough people to do the Bunny Trick". This line not only interests the crowd but brings back those few kids that were about to leave. (For heaven's sake, spring for the 3-D bunnies – the difference in reaction is amazing).

Whilst holding the person's hand and as I am about to reveal the baby bunnies, I pause and say, quite clearly and frankly... "By the way, folks, I do need to mention from time to time that I do work for tips. I am not paid by anyone except my audience, so if you feel my little act is worth a dollar or two...or 20, at any time, the kitty is here (indicate tip coffer). I will not mention it again... for several minutes."

Here's another little line I use once in a while: "To those of you who have been generous already, I thank you... To those of you who are about to be generous, I thank you... To those of you with no intention of being generous, may the good Lord bless you and keep you... somewhere near the juggler."

Sometimes I will end with the Bunny trick, or

perhaps continue to conclude with Professor's Nightmare or; if it warrants, add Linking Ropes with the three equal ropes from Professor's Nightmare. (Yes, a switch, of course. I use a change bag, which can then be used to collect tips.)

As you can see, this is anywhere from 8-10 minutes of simple yet effective and entertaining magic.

Now, if you hold the extended crowd too long, the ones who started with you may drift away to get to the movie on time, make their dinner reservations or get to that hot date, and the ones who just arrived have not yet seen enough to warrant a tip. Hence, be constantly aware of your crowd and suit the length of your act to their attention span.

Once you have completed your act and collected whatever tips come in, saying your thank-you's, (especially to the kids – a bent, stretched and engraved souvenir penny from them won't pay the rent but it sure lifts your spirits), this is a good time to size up your crowd: did most of them come in toward the middle or end of your act? If so, pick up from the beginning, and run the act again. See the earlier section pertaining to The Re-Hash. Perhaps have a couple of alternative effects you can use to start up.

Or, if the act has a specific end, I often say, "Thank you folks, I hope you enjoyed my little show. Any generosities you care to share will be gratefully accepted," and then add: "If you just got here or you could not get close enough to see what was going on, stick around; we will start all over momentarily."

From time to time you will have some kids who just do not go away, and by the time they have seen the show a few times they begin to take the lines, which throws off the timing. You can either take the WC Fields approach with "Pipe down, kid; I work alone," or, just let them do it, because they will anyway. In between sets just level with them, quietly, and let them know not to do that. Most often I have found they are understanding.

Occasionally you will get a crowd that enjoys the show and just walks away without tipping. Resist the temptation to react negatively. There can be many reasons for this: they do not have change (and may come back later), they tipped while you were not looking, they are poor, or possibly just obtuse.

Be gracious; you can afford to be. Resist the impulse to make snotty comments to those who do not tip. Remember, no one will come back and tip you because you called them a cheap SOB.

Once you have mastered the art of street performing, you can make a living pretty much anywhere in the world. If you like to travel, go for it: if you *have* traveled and learned some words, phrases, or more in various foreign languages, use them; they can help your tip pitch if you read your audience rightly.

Of course, figures can vary depending on the crowd or the economy, but performing an 8-10 minute act, turning the tip, and repeating, should garner you anywhere from $20-$50 an hour. As has been stated, three or four hours of this will beat the heck out of wages.

Working the street at Universal Studio's City Walk, Los Angeles

15. Taxes

Before you go trundling off without a thought to your dear old Uncle Sam, let me encourage you to reconsider your options. The day will come when you will want to buy a car, a boat, a house, New Jersey. Lenders have a hard time loaning thousands of dollars to someone whose tax records show that they only made $3.60 last year. Besides, you would miss the feeling of pride which goes along with supporting your government.

I suggest that you keep a day book with you and in addition to jotting down all of your expenses (for tax deductions, of course), write down daily how much you made, where and how long it took you to make it. At the end of the year, go over the book with your accountant and come to some equitable arrangement with the I.R.S. So you pay some taxes... BIG DEAL. Those Stealth Bombers don't grow on trees, y'know... You may want to put some percentage of your weekly take into a special coffee can in case the Governor wants a new limo. Beyond the tax help, your day book will give you a good account of what bars, days, and times are most profitable.

16. The Bottom Line

* Running a 10-20 minute routine through a crowded bar should net you around $20 - $40 per hour or more.

* Include a trick with a borrowed $5.00 bill and your take will rise.

* Borrowing $20 bills in the right watering holes can be glorious.

* As you can see, a 4 or 5 hour night can put well over $100 cash in your pocket.

* Three or four nights a week and you should have no trouble sporting the ladies to some champagne.

17. Alfie's Busking Vest

Save for the hat (used to collect tips), my most important piece of equipment is my vest. I highly recommend the use of a vest as it can do so many helpful things. First of all, the natural position of the thumbs in the pockets is useful for securing and ditching thumb tips. Divide the pockets into sections and you can store several tips in an upright position. (Make them deep enough that the tips do not fall out: it is disconcerting to realize, suddenly, that your $100 bill trick is somewhere on the floor of a crowded bar).

More importantly, the vest, properly rigged, is as invaluable as an invisible servant. As for mine, it is the simplest of the simple. It has a low cut scoop in the front: just below the scoop, I have sewn a black strip of material all the way across on the inside. This material hangs down four or five inches; enough to tuck inside the trouser waist band, creating a large, easily accessible pocket for getting rid of coins, thumb tips, dye tubes, color changing knives or a small miniature of the Queen.

It should not take you more than a half an hour to make up a lapping vest such as I have described. It will pay off over and over again and add to your reputation as a miracle worker.

18. Summary

You hold in your hand the blueprint to continuous cash

flow. With talent, charm and chutzpah you should be able to go out tonight and make a mockery of the pittance you shelled out for this manual.

My Personal Guarantee

If you do not, for any reason, make more than 10 times what you paid for *Busking as a Mercenary Art* on your very first night of busking, I will personally sympathize with you and wish you better luck on night two.

Now get out there and hustle!

ALFIE,
"KING OF THE STREET CONJURORS"
PRESENTS,

RESERVE STOCK
V.S.O.P.*

A Collection of six strong effects for the strolling magician, from one of magic's most popular buskers.

* VERY SPECIAL OLD PATTER

**RESERVE STOCK
V.S.O.P.***
**BY ALFIE,
"KING OF THE STREET CONJURORS"
AKA J. PAUL MOORE**

All rights reserved. No portion of this material may be reproduced in any form or by any means, without the express written permission from the author or his agent, not no how, not no way.

PRINTED IN THE UNITED STATES OF AMERICA – 2012

Copyright © 2012 by the author, J. Paul Moore

Ion Drive Publishing,
Los Angeles

http://IonDrivePublishing.com

Table of Contents

ForWord

Preface

1. 281 Words About Patter 1

2. A Little Blue Material 2

3. Seven Card Stop 6

4. From The Professor 12

5. The Eight-of-Clubs Trick 15

6. Yet Another Ambitious Card
   Routine 18

7. The Olympic Card Trick 20

8. Simple Pocket Tricks 22

9. Odds and Ends and Superfluous
   Babble 25

BackWord 29
Acknowledgements 31
Thanks To the Magic Castle 33
Three-Card Monte 35

ForWord

I've known Alfie for a long time... even from before he became Alfie. Over the years we have had many interesting discussions about magic. One thing we agree on is that magic doesn't have to be difficult to be good – but it does have to be entertaining.

If you've ever had the opportunity to see Alfie perform, you'd know by the gasps of amazement, the laughs of pleasure, and the applause of appreciation, that here is a man who knows what he is doing. This, in a nutshell, is Alfie. He's more than a magician – he's an entertainer.

— Jules Lenier

Preface

As a busker, one learns very quickly what is entertaining and what is being endured. Tips do not come from people who are politely putting up with your efforts. Conversely, money flows from those who are truly amazed, amused and entertained.

Contained within are a half-dozen powerful effects which have served me well over my years as a strolling magician. In addition, I have included suggestions of several under-rated pocket tricks which should not be passed over simply because they are easy or old. I make no claim at originality other than my own specific handling and patter. Where memory serves I have noted the originator or source of the basic effect.

As this volume is intended for the experienced magician I shall not dwell overly long on specific moves other than to name the sleight involved. Where moves need to be timed to specific patter I shall elaborate as clarity dictates.

If your intention is to make a few bucks strolling miracles through a saloon or supper club, I am certain you will find these effects and presentations helpful. Best of luck!

FLOAT A BORROWED BILL AND IT MAY COME YOUR WAY!

- ALFIE,
AKA J. Paul Moore

1. 281 Words About Patter

Among your magical talents, think of yourself as a storyteller. Few presentations are as boring as the "Now I'm gonna..." approach, where the magician basically describes what he/she is doing. "Now I'm gonna have you take a card... Now I'm gonna have you put it back... Now I'm gonna shuffle the cards..." If this is the kind of thing that you are contemplating, STOP! Get a job. Be a collaborating consultant or an absentee board member. Magic is not your bag. You are not entertaining anyone and you are not going to make any money.

You must weave a story around what you are doing. You are creating an illusion, not baking muffins. Make it bigger than life. Use exotic references, colorful allusions... "My guide and I were closing in on a group of Pygmies just south of Rangoon when I spotted this knife lying in the weeds beside the trail..." (opening for a color-changing knife routine). "Not a half-mile from the Silk Gardens of Tai Wee I encountered a merchant selling scarves..." (opening a silk routine). Make it believable or preposterous or amusing or spellbinding, but weave a storyline of interest and you will be well-rewarded.

I certainly expect that your own genius will con-jure up your own brilliant patter. I include my own evolved patter only as an example of how important the story-line is to the effects presented. Feel free to use any or all of it if you so desire but you will be better- served to unleash your own creative force to make each effect uniquely your own.

I cannot say too much about the importance of patter but I probably already have. Do not deny your-self the joy of creating effective interesting patter.

2. A LITTLE BLUE MATERIAL

This is the silk which jumps from hand to hand as described in most any beginning thumb tip book. I first saw it performed by John Pedan, a magician in Scots' attire at the Renaissance Pleasure Faire in California.

(Blue silk in tip, tip on right thumb)... **"You seem like a worldly crowd. You don't mind a little blue material, do you? Good. Let us begin, then, with a materialization using only the elements in the air..."** (looking into the air, reach up with your right hand and appear to pluck an invisible element from the air)... **"A little bit of this,"** (look into the air to your left and repeat the move with your left hand), **"and a little bit of that..."** (as you say this, and under cover of the misdirection, slip the tip off and into your closing right fist; suiting the action to the word, say.)... **"That goes into this,"** (wave fingers) **"and you materialize, out of the blue, *blue material!*"** (Pluck silk partly out of tip for all to see)... **"Material is the best thing for a materialization..."** (pull silk out and flourish with left hand as you slip the tip back on to right thumb; display silk with both hands, keeping tip behind silk). **"Now this is a little wrinkled, but it's old material; I wrote it years ago."** (Holding silk between the tipped thumb and fingers of right hand, draw the silk across the palm of your open left hand; reverse direction and draw silk across the closing palm of your left hand, leaving tip in closed left fist, and pull silk free with a flourish). **"Now I shall cause the material to de-materialize from my left hand..."** (tucking silk partly into tip with some sticking out), **"and rematerialize in my right hand."** (Show right hand empty front and back). **"I could do it the other way, it's... immaterial."** (Tuck silk into tip, withdraw, and continue to seem to tuck silk into left hand with fore and middle finger: this is merely a subtlety so that the last digit out of your hand is not your thumb). **"Keep one eye on this hand..."** (move left hand up and to your left, and at the same time and under cover of this misdirection, slip tip from right thumb and close fist around it), **"and one eye on this hand..."** (move right hand up and to the right; bring fists together with a bump and a *Shazam!* and separate them again; look somewhat smug and self-satisfied). **"Sure enough, it's gone from here and reappears over here..."** (do not open hands). **"The tricky part is to get it to go back..."** (as old as this bit is, it still gets, at the very least, a chuckle; open your left hand in a gesture toward the person or area which reacted as you say), **"You don't trust me, do you? I don't blame you, I wouldn't either. See, here it is, over here."** (Pull silk free of right hand and flourish as you slip right thumb back into the tip; grasp silk with right thumb and fingers and repeat pull-through move, leaving tip in left closed fist; immediately begin to tuck silk into tip as you say), **"The nice thing about this effect is, when you are done, you merely tuck it back into the left hand, open a small door in the air, say *Open Sesame*,"** (suit the action to the words by reaching forward and up into the air: mime the opening of a small door), **"put it away, close the door,"** (do so with a casual slap with the right hand) **"and the trick is over..."** (gesture up and out with both hands).

Take your time with this routine. Smooth and flowing is the key, not speed. Self consciousness and fear of discovery is, of course, the biggest bugaboo about using a thumb tip. Relax. Only those who already know the trick will see the tip, and even at that they will not really see it.

SIDEBAR – Clark, 'The Senator', Crandall was giving a lecture at the Magic Castle some decades ago when he did the cigarette-in-the-hanky trick. After finishing, he asked the magicians, "Does anyone know how I did that?" The magi looked a bit sheepish and indicated that he had used a thumb tip. The Senator then asked, "Did you see it?" "Well, yes," they replied. "What color was it" asked Crandall. "Flesh colored" they replied. At which point The Senator held up the silver thumb tip he had been using (the old metal thumb tip with the paint stripped off). The point being that even if you know the gaff, it is invisible if you do it right.

FOR THE KIDS

Although this routine works well with most ages, I find a simpler routine with **"Look here. Watch. Look now it's over here. Oh, oh, all gone,"** patter works very well with very young (2 to 5 years) children often encountered in a restaurant situation. It is visual, colorful, simple, and easy to follow. The parents will be thrilled, and quite possibly generous if you delight their child.

WORK TO THE KIDS: THEY WILL LOVE IT, THE PARENTS WILL BE GENEROUS, AND YOU MAY PICK UP A BIRTHDAY PARTY...

3. SEVEN- CARD STOP

This is one of the strongest card effects in my arsenal. It is based on a psychological force detailed in mentalist genius Ted Annaman's books, on sale at secret book stores everywhere. It is a magnificent force and will assure your reputation as a miracle worker. I have expanded on the basic idea to utilize two spectators, at least one of them a lady, if possible. The reason for this is only that I prefer to work with a lady's hand.

Select a lady from the audience and bring her to your left. Select a gentleman and bring him to your right. After a bit of improvisational banter, have them each take a card at random and show it to the audience. Have them returned to the deck and bring them to the seventh and eighth position from the top using your favorite method.

Just in case you do not have a favorite method, here is the one I use:

While cards are being shown, casually overhand shuffle the deck at random. Say, **"Everybody help remember the cards..."** Run off three cards into your left hand as you say, **"If I come to the end of the trick,"** (gesture with the bulk of the deck in your right hand as you say), **"and you don't know what the cards are,"** (pause)... **"it's boring."** Run two more cards as you say, **"Especially for me."** Pause and gesture again with the bulk of the deck as you say, **"Do you know how many times I have seen this trick?"** (Run one more card and pretend to run a few more; interrupt yourself and hold out the six cards in your left hand)... **"Return your card, face down; if you put it face up, a mime could find it."** Turn to the second spectator... **"Face down... the card, I mean."** Continue to casually overhand-shuffle the cards into your left hand as you say, **"Late at night, you get a lot of that face-down stuff..."** Look at the lady on your left... **"I see you are skeptical: I'll shuffle them again..."** (Casually overhand-shuffle the cards again, running the last 10 or so cards)... **"Honestly shuffled... no funny business... that's why you're not laughing."**

Note: When you have done this control many times you will develop a sense of where to run the cards and when you can drop the last packet of five or six cards, adding a little more casualness to the shuffle.

At this point you have an apparently shuffled deck in your left hand with the selected cards at the seventh and eighth position from the top.

Address the lady on your left... **"Would you hold out your magic hand, with the palm side up?"** (You will be surprised at how often, in an adult crowd, her date or husband will say, "That's not her magic hand;" I suggest you leave this comment alone and move on). Wave your hand or wand over her hand and chant... **"Nam myoho renge keo, Timothy Leary, brown rice, spare change, L. Ron Hubbard, Anthony Robbins... It's my own personal mantra. I got it from the Maharishi Hashish Yogi, back in the sixties."**

Aside from being mildly amusing, this banter is designed to give the audience time to forget any suspicions they may have to this point, and most importantly, allows the lady to get a little tired of holding her hand out.

This is the Anneman psychological force part of the trick. Begin to put cards, one at a time, from the top of the deck into the lady's hand at a moderate and even pace. DO NOT COUNT OUT LOUD. As you lay down the fifth card, without stopping say somewhat impatiently, **"Well, say *stop* somewhere!"** and keep laying cards down. Nearly ninety percent of the time she will say *stop* while the seventh card is either in your hand or in hers, or on top of the deck. I will describe the ideal scenario and later add a variety of get-outs in case things go awry.

At the risk of being redundant again, let me describe the scene at this point: you have a spectator to your right and a lady to your left holding seven cards in her hand with a selected card on top. You have the remainder of the deck in your left hand with the other selected card on top. Picking the top card from the lady's hand you say, **"If the card you stopped on turns out to be one of the selected cards, you've done a pretty good trick,"** (turn the card face up for all to see; get ready for a top change), **"Whose card?"** (Gesture with your left [deck] hand toward the person on your right saying), **"Is it yours?"** (Under cover of this gesture, execute your top change; if it is their card, turn back to your left; if it is not, turn back anyway and establish that the lady has found her own card; gesturing with the face-down card in your right hand, say), **"This was a fair choice, was it not? You did not have to stop here, you could have stopped here..."** (indicate top card of the deck in your left hand). **"Do you know what would have happened then?"** (Execute a one-handed turnover of the card as you say), **"I would have cheated... It still would have been your card."** There should be a nice reaction here, and then they will begin to suspect the other card; turn it over as you say, **"Of course, *this* would have been your card!"**

Often at this point applause will ensue. If so stop there and acknowledge their reaction.

Sometimes they will remain in stunned silence, so finish up by displaying all cards face-up, saying, **"And of course all these cards are different; as long as you know this, it's just a question of going home and practicing."**

Just as I might suggest you do a couple of credential-establishing card tricks before this, I also suggest this as a closer. It is hard to top.

THE GET-OUTS

There are a few variables in this trick and you should be prepared to deal with them.

A. The Lady Stops on the Eighth Card

Set the bulk of the deck down and pick up the packet from her hand. Reveal the eighth card and top change to the seventh under the same patter and gestures as already suggested.

B. The Lady Does Not Stop Until You Are Way Past The Cards

When you are well past the cards (tenth or twelfth) mutter, without stopping, **"You are familiar with the** word?" Wherever she now stops, you say, **"Now I said something there, did I influence you in any way? I will give you one opportunity to change your mind. You may go a little further, you may go back or you may stay here."** Sometimes she will go back to the area you need. Sometimes she will go further. If she goes further, try... **"I like a lady who goes a little further."** Wherever you end up, say, **"You could have taken any number of cards, and you nearly did. Do you know how many cards you took? Did you count? Nor did I. I'd say there were about seventeen. Let's see..."** Very deliberately and openly count the cards, without reversing their order, and secure a break above the eighth card; continue counting the cards and square up the deck as you comment, **"Seventeen; actually, I *did* count..."** (Look at audience). **"Out of any number between one and forty-eight that she might have taken, she chose the number seventeen..."** (Look at the spectator on your right; get ready to pass back to the eighth card). **"I'm not playing with a full deck. I should have told you that at the beginning..."** (Turn back to the lady and execute your best pass as you say), **"You probably knew that from the beginning."** You are now set to continue as aforementioned.

C. You Turn The Cards Over And They Are Wrong
Consider the ITT Institute, DeVry, or perhaps the

Peace Corps. (Do we still have a Peace Corps?) Practice your control.

Although it takes a great deal of space to detail the workings of this routine, in execution it is only about three to four minutes in length, including the get-out.

4. FROM THE PROFESSOR

As a fledgling magician in the mid-sixties, and through my career and into the present, I have had the honor, privilege, and good fortune to be a member of the world-famous Magic Castle in Hollywood, California.

I watched in awe as Jay Ose amazed the Close-up Gallery and Dai Vernon held court in his corner. I learned from incredible magicians like Slydini, Francis Carlyle, Johnny Platt, and even a certain surly Italian magician who would be angry if I even mentioned his name.

One late evening in the mid-eighties, a young magician approached Dai Vernon in the main bar and asked what he thought about his color-change, which he demonstrated, as most magicians might, by passing his hand over the deck. **"No, no!"** cried the Professor.

"That's all wrong. The card should never leave their sight. Look, look, give me the cards! Look, look (cigar ashes tumbling), **the card should *never* leave their sight. Look, just wave your hand. Spread your fingers. Look, I'll do it again."**

For about five minutes he demonstrated this "Vernon Touch," which elevated a good effect to a visual miracle. For the specific handling, I would refer you to his book, *The Vernon Touch*.

The following routine will work with whatever color change you use, but I strongly suggest you check out the Professor's.

Select a spectator on your left and have them take a card, show it, and return it to the deck face-down, **"If you put it face-up, a mime could find it... Okay, maybe not a mime."** Shuffle the cards, ending up with the selected card on top. Hold the deck, face up, in your left hand. Gesture to audience with your open right hand... **"Did you all see the selected card?"**

Relax your right hand to rest on the deck for a moment. Gesture with your right hand to the spectator on your left... **"Did you look at the card yourself?"**

Under cover of this movement and patter, push the top card, which is nearest your left palm, off the front of the deck with your left forefinger, and into your gesturing right hand. Drop your hand casually to your right side. Bring your hand back up and point to the face-up deck in your left hand. (Keep that little finger tucked in, and don't flag your thumb). **"You did not select the four of hearts. A proper magician could wave his hand,"** (do so and drop the card on the deck, quickly spreading your fingers wide, and vibrating your hand – the effect is startling)... **"and the card would change."**

Pause for a moment while the cries of "Witch! Witch! Burn him!" die down.

The Expose

This next bit not only satisfies the audience's desire to see the trick again, but it gets a good chuckle, and disarms those who thought they were following the modus-operandi.

Still holding the deck face up in your left hand, you continue. **"There are a couple of ways you can do this if you would like to work it into your own routine."** Bring your right hand up to cover the selected card showing on the bottom of the deck. Hold the deck from the ends with the right hand. **"While no one is looking, secretly palm off the selected card and keep it in your right hand..."** (under cover of this patter make it appear that you are, somewhat obviously, palming off the selected card, but in reality and under the full cover of your right hand, simply slip the card to the top of the deck; even the sound will add to the illusion that you are palming the card)... **"and drop it on the deck."** Pause... Gesture openly with your right hand as you say, **"I don't do it that way, but that is a way it could be done."**

Take advantage of the reaction to relax your right hand back to the deck. Look to the spectator on your left and use the exact same palming move you used at the beginning, under cover of the gesture and the line of, **"If you really want to practice..."** (point to the four of hearts), **"keep it under the four of hearts... palm off the four,"** (lay the selected card on the deck and make it appear that you are, again, obviously palming off a card)... **"revealing the selected card."** Pause a moment, then gesture openly with your empty right hand, saying, **"I don't use that method either: I prefer magic... you don't have to practice."**

5. THE EIGHT-OF-CLUBS TRICK

Among the many great magicians from whom I learned was Francis Carlyle, certainly a master of the classic force. He would corner me in the Blackstone Room at the Castle and continually force cards on me. He would classic-force all four aces and then do it again face-up. His advice was, "Always classic-force the card, whether you need it or not. This gives you constant practice and the opportunity to get good. If the spectator takes the force, do a force trick; if they do not take it, do a different trick. The audience does not know what you are going to do until you have done it.

The following effect and get-out is an excellent ice breaker when the force works, and a good trick when it does not.

After having the deck examined and shuffled by the spectator, glimpse your force card. In this example we will say it is the eight of clubs... Say, **"Have you ever seen the Eight-of-Clubs trick? I'll show you; it's just a quick trick."** (Classic-force the eight of clubs)... **"Take out a card; this is the fastest trick I do... in fact, it's over..."** (said as they take the card from the deck, displaying the eight of clubs for all to see)... **"Some folks say the Eight-of-Clubs trick is too quick: you don't have time to enjoy it."** If they do not commit to the force card, leave out this line.

When this works, which is most of the time if you get good at the classic force, it is a good laugh and rather impressive. When it does not, do this:

THE GET-OUT

While the spectator is looking at their card, cut the force card (eight of clubs) to the top of the deck, have the selected card returned on top, cut it to the center, and shuffle ending up with the eight of clubs second from the top and the selected card on top. All during your shuffling and attendant finger flinging, patter somewhat smugly, **"You can see why its called the Eight-of-Clubs trick: your card remains under my control at all times. Even though I shuffle and cut the cards, it takes but a wave of the hand and a snap of the fingers and your card, the eight of clubs, rises to the top of the deck."** Execute a double lift and proudly display the eight of clubs, saying, **"Your card, the eight of clubs."** Turn the double face down on the deck and appear to be moving on to another effect. Let the spectator interrupt you with **"That's not my card."** (Remember, audiences are polite and may not say anything so you may have to coax them.)

Looking somewhat puzzled, pick up the top card, and looking at it (but not showing it) you say, **"You didn't take the eight of clubs? Didn't I mention this was the Eight-of-Clubs trick? Well, you've taken the wrong card! Fortunately it's a magic trick."** Put the (correct) card in their hand and hand them the magic wand. **"Wave the wand over the** card and say Abra-ca-whatzit -- and it changes into your card." Hold the deck in such a way that the spectator must slide the card off the front edge. As they slide the top card off, the second card will slide forward a little, setting itself up for an easy palming. As the spectator is looking at his card, palm off the eight of clubs. Have them put their card on the deck, face down. Have them wave their hand again, and say, **"Eight of clubs."** As you demonstrate, drop the eight of clubs on top of the deck ala the Vernon Touch Color Change. Say, **"Take a look."** Let the spectator turn the card over and show it. Say, **"It changes back to the eight of clubs... That's why its called the Eight-of-Clubs trick,"** as you casually overhand-shuffle the cards.

6. Yet Another Ambitious Card Routine

Surely another ambitious card routine is not high on the list of things needed in the world of magic. I include this one, not to make the book bigger as some may suspect, but because it is a nice audience participation effect, and falls into the expose category.

After you have done a few card tricks and in response to the question, "How did you do that?" you say, displaying the cards face up and then face down, **"To tell you the truth, it does not matter which card you take. If it mattered, I wouldn't give you a choice."** Here, pick up the top card, but do not show it... **"I'd say, here; this is your card, and then 1'd just put it on top so I'd know where it is..."** (Put the card back on top and get ready to execute a triple lift). **"Let's say, for example, that you *did* take the top card,"** (execute your triple and show the face, the six of diamonds), **"say, the six of diamonds."** Turn the triple lift face down on the deck. **"All I have to do is keep it on top. Most people will not put their card on top. Most will put it somewhere in the middle."** Take top card, without showing, and put it somewhere in the middle... **"Do not let this bother you, merely turn the deck end for end,"** (do so), **"wave your hand, snap your fingers, and the six of diamonds rises back to the top of the deck."** Execute a double lift showing the 6 of diamonds. **"Perhaps 1 went a little fast: I'll slow it down."** Turn the double face down on the deck; run your thumb down the edge of the deck and instruct the spectator to say *stop* anywhere. Wherever they stop, insert the top card at this point and square the deck. Handing the spectator the deck... **"You can do it yourself: hold the deck in your own hand. Turn the deck end-for-end, wave your hand, and snap your fingers... The six of** diamonds rises back to the top of the deck. Take a look. See, anyone can do this stuff."

Addendum

If you would like to "gild the lily" on this, you could do the first two reveals yourself and then do a top change to set up the final phase where the spectator seems to do the trick.

7. The Olympic Card Trick

A good follow-up trick, this one is very visual and requires only one and a half sleights.

Having had a card selected, returned, and controlled to the top of the deck, set the deck down and say something to the effect of, **"This is the Olympic Card Trick. Please cut the cards into three relatively even packs. They don't have to be exact, but close."** Once this is done, name the three packs as Gold, Silver and Bronze, with the force pack (the one with the selected card on top) as the Silver, preferably in the middle. (Having it in the middle is not critical, but helpful).

The following patter executes the *Magician's Choice*, bringing you to the Silver packet. Turn to a male, other than the person who selected the card, and say, **"Gold, Silver, and Bronze; name one of the three."** About 80% of the time, a man will say "Silver," believing the Gold and Bronze on the ends are too obvious. (A woman will almost always say "Gold"... Sorry, ladies, 'tis true). If the gentleman says "Silver," continue, **"The selected card will leap from the Silver packet, do a double Greek somersault in mid-air, and land face-up on the table."** Pick up the Silver packet from the ends with the fingers and thumb of the right hand. With the left thumb and under cover of the right hand slide the top card approximately a half-inch to the right. Hold the pack about one foot above the table with your right hand and drop it with a hearty *Shazam!* or some such clever punctuation. The air current on the deck will cause the top offset card to turn over and appear face-up on the pack as the pack hits the table. (This phenomenon does not work consistently with a full deck of cards, hence the cutting of the cards into three packs).

THE ALTERNATIVES

If the gentleman names either Gold or Bronze, immediately pick up that pack and turn to another person and say **"Silver or Bronze for you?"** If they pick Bronze, pick it up, put it with the Gold, and set them both aside, saying to the person who selected the card, **"You have won the Silver Medal; your card will leap..."** If the second person says "Silver," pick it up, and, holding the Gold in one hand and the Silver in the other, turn to the person who selected the card, who should be facing you. Holding out both packets, say to that person, **"You selected the card... Left or Right?"** Whichever they say, drop the neutral pack to the side saying, **"Your card will leap from the Silver packet."** (Because the spectator is facing you, the choice of Left or Right could either be your left or their left, whichever is needed.

8. Simple Pocket Tricks

Just because a trick is easy, cheap or even old hat, it will still work well for you as a filler or change of pace. Once you have established your credentials as a sleight-of-hand artist, there is no reason why you cannot slip in a few over-the-counter tricks. While the list of good pocket tricks is long, I would mention a few that have served me well. Usually these come with perfectly satisfactory patter lines on which you may expand, exercising your own creative genius.

1. Multiplying Rabbits

Perhaps more effective than a sponge ball routine in that it uses "cute little bunnies". Often someone will ask, "Can you pull a rabbit out of your hat?" What better entree could you ask for? This trick is not only wonderful for kids, but goes down great with ladies.

2. Hopping Half

A very effective, amusing and simple coin routine that can be reset in your pocket as you are moving through the crowd.

3. Invisible Deck / Brain Wave

Either do a deck-switch, or just do this one trick as a part your re-hash and then put it away and move on to something else.

4. Mental Photography

An incredibly visual, baffling, and simple effect for all ages. Present it with a "Here is a trick you could pick up at the Magic Shop and do for *your* friends..." Make no secret of the fact that it is a specially designed deck, just do not actually reveal the secret itself.

5. Hot Rod, or Fantastik

An almost indestructible piece of equipment that takes up little room in your pocket, weighs nearly nothing, does not need to be re-set, and sparkles brilliantly in the sun. I suggest you carry two or more so you can repeat the trick later with a different color. This effect usually comes with just the basic working instructions.

Here is the patter I use:

Displaying the unit, **"I have here six precious gems set in an ebony wand... or six chips of glass on a plastic stick, depending on how fanciful you want to be about it. Give us a number between one and six, as there are six colors. Three; very well: one, two, three, brings you to the diamond. I might have known. Watch: one, two, three..."** (move). **"They all change to the diamonds you selected..."** (Do the move to show diamonds on both sides; do not over-prove this). **"Shake it once,"** (do the move), **"and they all come back on this side and remain diamond on this side. Shake it twice and they come back on both sides,"** (do the move). **"But since you asked for diamonds, I shall leave it,"** (do move) **"with the diamond on this side, all six colors on the other side, and you can take a look at it if you like."** (Hand unit out for examination). **"Please don't break the switch... Just joking about the switch. Did i mention that you have to be a magician to do it?"**

(For children under 6 years of age, ask them their age and use that number).

9. Odds and Ends and Superfluous Babble

Re-Hashing

Once you have completed your standard routine and collected your tips, you may want to continue with this same group. For this purpose, you may want to consider the following:

      1. Three-Shell Game
      2. Three-Card Monte
      3. Endless Chain
      4. Poker Deals
      5. Gambling Exposé

Carry some play-money, or better yet, copy off some fake bills with your picture and telephone number. Give these out for your patrons to gamble with, and be sure not to win them all back. If you do not have bills, use sugar packs or tooth picks. Your audience will have more fun if they can actually bet on your games.

Fillers

At the risk of being redundant, yet again, let me state that once you have established your credentials you can fill out some time with some simple effects. For example:

1. Have half a dozen or so cards selected, returned to the deck, one at a time, shuffling in between. Finger fling a little and have the folks hold out their hand. Rapidly deal out the selected cards to the proper hands.

2. If you feel confident, **let the audience make up a card trick** and find your advantages as you go along. Who should shuffle? Who would you like to take a card? Try to force it and you are home free. Palm the card out if opportunity allows. Glimpse the card. Control it. Reverse it. Slip it to the bartender or waitress. You will be pleasantly surprised at how little it takes to turn an apparently legitimate improvisation into a minor miracle.

3. Bar Bets abound in a wide variety of publications. Pick out a few and add them to your routine. Even though you may not make bets with them, your patrons will appreciate learning them so they can cheat their friends out of their life savings. (Check out Harry Anderson's books).

4. BE AWARE! Keep your eyes open for opportunities. The dimly lit bar or busy restaurant is custom-made for the observant trickster.

I sincerely hope that this small tome will not only provide you with some good material, but will also inspire you to experiment and create miracles.

ON THE COVER

I created the character of ALFIE, "King of the Street Conjurors" for the first annual Great Dickens Christmas Fair, circa 1970. After the Fair I took the character into the streets of San Francisco, becoming one of the first of The City's Street Performers, where I met an artist named Paula. We spent some time together and she painted the cover portrait in oils. Said portrait now hangs somewhere in the Magic Castle, in Hollywood (or perhaps Milt's garage). I lost contact with Paula (whose last name I do not remember) somewhere along the line, so, Paula, if you see this please contact me.

Acknowledgements

Does anyone ever read the acknowledgments other than the acknowledged? I hope so, because there are a good many folk who have helped me get this book up and running. At the top of the list is, of course, my publisher, Ion Drive Publishing, under the guidance of R. Merlin, and their most talented staff, Jacque Mahoney and Rain Livengood, as well as the lovely Vannassa Murphy, who sees to our heath & nutrition.

Also, although I do not have room to list them all, I thank the magicians, staff and crew of The Magic Castle who inspired, guided and taught me the principles of performance magic which have kept me solvent and occasionally wealthy throughout my career.

Finally I would like to thank Geno & Penny Munari, owners of Houdini Magic for hiring me as a pitchman for their Las Vegas magic shops as well as the Main Street Magic Shop in Disneyland. Learning the art of the pitch furthered my performance level immensely.

And, of course, I would like to thank the thousands of folk who have dropped a couple of bucks into my hat.

With a Special Thank You to
Bill and Milt Larson,
Creators of

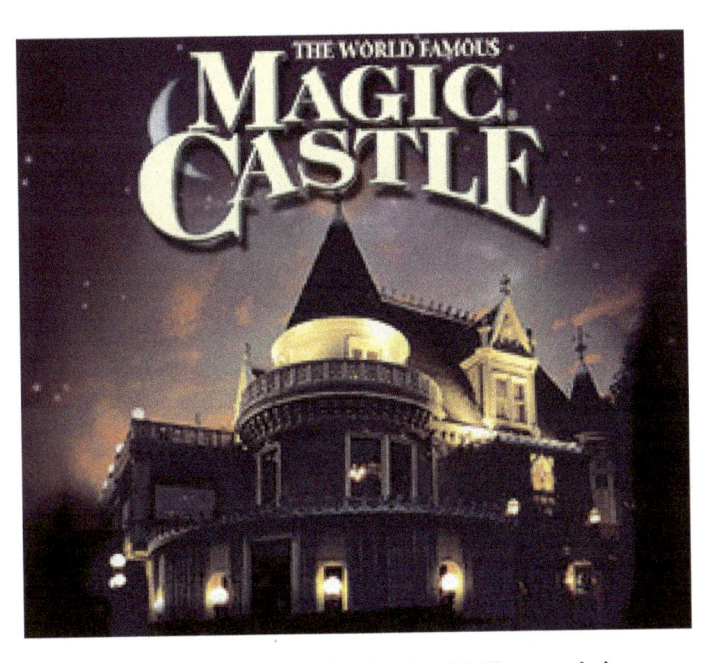

The world famous Magic Castle in Hollywood is my alma mater; there I learned the techniques and art of performance magic from the masters of the age, such as Dai Vernon, Jay Ose, Francis Carlyle, Slydini, Johnny Platt, Billy McComb, Jules Lenier, and a long list of legends.

Long Live the Magic Castle!

SELLING SOMETHING

Although I pitched and sold magic for many years with Houdini Magic, I personally have never had much acumen for selling things in the Street situation. Many do however, and selling trick decks (Svengalli, Mental Photography, Stripper Decks, etcetera) or a variety of simple effects can lift you to the upper income brackets (for street performers).

I have incorporated a simple instructional packet on the

Three Card Monte which I offer, for a pittance, after I have demonstrated the old swindle. I find the Monte appeals to everyone from the back alleys to the board room and am constantly amazed at how many people do not know this much-exposed scam.

Patter: **"Now, we are not going to play for real money, that is against the law; but I have come prepared to stake you to a solid gold-colored plastic coin"**

The game is much more fun and effective if the Mark has something to wager. If you are in the area for a while and seeking gigs, make up a miniature $20 bill with your picture & contact information. Included here is the instructional packet I sold. Feel free to copy it and sell it yourself.

Decades ago, when I was working The Magic Cellar in San Francisco, I had the pleasure of meeting an actual Grifter from the 30's who told me, "When you really need money right away, sell information." A few sheets of paper cost nearly nothing and you can sell them for a quick buck (or more).

You might also consider "Pitching the Mouse", a small plastic mouse that appears to crawl all over your hand. I expect you can still find them in any carnival supply store.

CONGRATULATIONS, you hold in your hand yet another method of fleecing your friends out of their excess capital. Allow me to redundantly reiterate, once again: "The Cheaters are often beaten severely about the head and shoulders by the Cheatees. N'uff said?

FOR ENTERTAINMENT PURPOSES ONLY!

Preface

Let me begin by stating that the Three Card Monte is not easy, like the Three Shell Game or the Endless Chain. Although the sleight involved is not terribly complicated, it must be perfected before the Monte becomes presentational. **I encourage you to practice this and all close-up effects in front of a mirror so you can see what the audience sees.** Watch your hands, at first to get the movements right, then, as you get comfortable, begin to watch to see how the subtleties play from the front.

Once *the move* and *the variant* become instinctual, you will begin to explore the psychological intricacies of this guessing game. There is always a winning card on the table. It is up to you to make sure it is not where the mark thinks it is. Sometimes that will be right where it is supposed to be, sometimes not. Your ongoing ability to **read the player** will dictate when and where to put the winning card.

Although the game is best played with a ***Shill*** (one of the supposed players who is actually, secretly, on your side), most likely you will be "throwing the Monte" on your own. For the purposes of enlightenment only, I will briefly outline the job description of:

The Grifter

This amiable rascal, much romanticized by Hollywood, was the low-down, S.O.B who made his living by exploiting human weakness and cheating people out of their hard earned money. (See the film, *The Flim-Flam Man,* with George C. Scott). The Grifter had to be good at the game, good at reading the players, and often, good at getting out of town quickly.

The Shill

In the desperate days when the Monte was played for real money, the Shill was an important ingredient in the scam. The Shill is, first of all, a secret confederate of the person "throwing the Monte" ie: the Grifter. Acting as a part of the crowd, he or she makes bets according to the needs of the Grifter. Sometimes it will be on the right card to lure marks in; sometimes it will be on the wrong card to throw them off. The Shill reads the signals from the Grifter as to where the red card is or where the Grifter wants the Shill to wager. The Shill is also the one who sets up the *bent-corner blow-off* at the end, which I shall cover later.

The Signals

Of course, any signals worked out between the Grifter and the Shill will work, however, this is one of the simplest. If the card is on your left, rest your right hand on the table. If it is on the right, rest your left hand on the table. If it is in the middle, rest both hands or no hands on the table.

The Lookout

Another important ingredient of the Monte was *The Lookout.* After all, the game is illegal and should the Constable on Patrol happen by, the Grifter and the players need some warning. Even more important, the Lookout (or Lookouts) keep an eye on the players. If the crowd begins to turn ugly, or should some

Mark win too much, the Lookout can instigate a diversion such as, "Beat it, the Bulls", "Cheese it, the Cops" or some such colorful phrase, thus instilling panic, disorder and chaos in the crowd, during which time the Shill or the Grifter (most likely the Shill) will grab all the money on the table (usually a cardboard box or inverted trash can) and make off through all the confusion. If it is the Shill, the Grifter can continue to work the neighborhood another day, utilizing, of course, a new Shill. The Lookout, the Shill and other confederates in the crowd also act as body guards for the Grifter in case a fight should break out when the Marks lose money, especially if they begin to think they have been cheated.

The Handling

The Move

Any three cards can be used as long as two are of one color and one is of a different color. Gently bend the cards slightly in the middle along the top to bottom line. This will "tent" the cards so that they can be easily picked up from the table. Lay the three cards, face down, on the table in a row from left to right: BLACK - RED - BLACK. Pick up the right hand card (black) with your right hand, holding the card face down, lengthwise between your thumb and middle finger-tips. Pick up the middle card (red) between the thumb and third finger of the same hand that is holding the black card. You are now holding one black card and one red card, face down in your right hand with the red card on the bottom, being held between the thumb and third finger tips. Moving your hand slightly to your left, toss the red card, face down onto the table a little to your left maintaining the black card in its position between the thumb and middle finger tips. Pick it up and do it again. Do this several times until you have a comfortable toss.

The Variant

Pick up the same two in the same fashion, and this time toss the black card from between the thumb and middle finger tips while retaining the red in its position between the thumb and third finger tips. This is *The Variant* and must be practiced until your hand and movement appear the same no matter which card you toss.

---------------------- Keep practicing, I'll wait ----------------------

Now that you are comfortable doing that...

The Third Card

We shall assume you have practiced the foregoing and are now ready to add the third card (the black card to your left). Pick the card up with the thumb and middle finger-tips of your left hand and gently toss it to the right of the table-top. Pick it up and do it again. Do this several times...

The Pattern

Hold the red and black cards in your right hand, as practiced.

Pick up the black card, as practiced, in your left hand. Gently toss the red card face-down onto the table to your left; gently toss the black card in your left hand face-down onto the table to your right, and finally toss the remaining black card in your right hand, face down to the table between the other two cards. You have ended up with the red card on the left, a black in the middle and a black on the right. Do it again and...

PLAYING THE GAME

You can now *Throw the Monte,* putting the odd card wherever you want. You can make it look like it is in one place when it is not. Work out a routine where you throw the cards legitimately as you demonstrate. Let the Mark win a few times to build up his confidence and perhaps encourage others to believe you are really "not very good at this game". When you feel the moment is right, throw the variant. – Play the psychological factor – The more you play, the better you will get.

PRACTICE THIS **A LOT!**

Now that you can do all that smoothly, practice the same thing but this time toss the black card from the right hand to the left, the black card from left to right and finally the red card to the middle, between the two black cards. If you have become proficient in this move, the spectator should now believe the red card to be on your left when it is actually in the middle. As you learn the psychology of the game you will begin to develop a sense of when to use the variant and when to play it straight.

A Subtlety

Some people actually watch, and may notice which fingers are holding which cards, so try this: as you toss the top card (black) to your left hand, move the middle finger down to the red card and release the third finger. This will add to the illusion that you tossed the bottom (red) card.

The Bent-Corner Blow-Off

Whereas the basic sleight for Throwing the Monte is relatively easy to learn, the ***bent-corner*** will take intense practice over a long period of time; however, it is well worth the time invested as it gets a great reaction at the end. (Unless, of course, you are really trying to cheat someone out of their money and then they may damage you).

After several throws in which your Marks have either won or lost, (most of them will have lost), you amiably announce that you want them to win a little something so you will show them what they are doing wrong. Picking up the red card between the thumb on the face and the first two fingers on the back, touch the upper right corner of the red card onto the face of the black card laying, face up, to your right on the table. As you say, "Do not watch the black cards"…tap the black card with the upper right hand corner of the red card a couple of times, move over to the other black card laying face-up on the table and repeat the action as you say, "Do not watch either of the black cards, only watch the red card." Toss it, face-up onto the table between the two black cards. What you have accomplished in this action is to slightly bend up the upper right hand corner of the red card. Your Marks, who should be watching intently by now, will notice that the red card is *slightly* bent. Relying on the W.C. Fields saying, "You cannot cheat an honest man," you can now count on most of your Marks to be ready to cheat you. Pick up the black card in your right hand and as you pick up the black card in your left hand (and while eyes are on your left hand), use your little finger to slightly bend the upper right hand corner of the black card. Finally, pick up the red card in your right hand. Execute the Variant and as you are tossing the black card in your left hand to the right, use the little finger of the right hand to bend the upper right hand corner of the red card back to its normal position and toss it down on the table to the middle. You now have the bent black card on your left, the unbent red card in the middle and the third card (unbent black) is on your right.

The hook is baited… wait for the fish to bite.

"You cannot cheat an honest man."
– W. C. Fields